AF342003

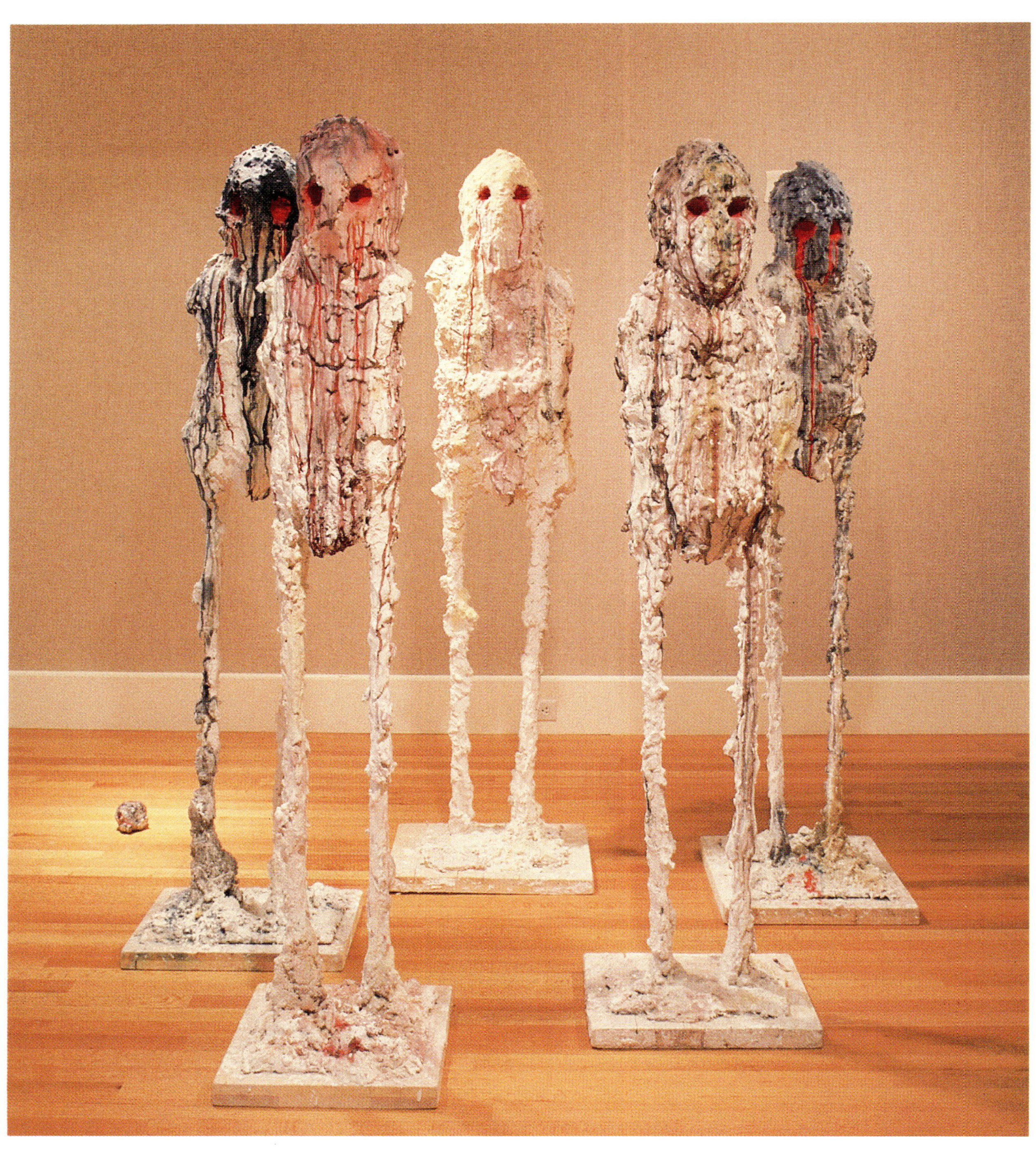

1. ***Figures with Bleeding Eyes,*** 1986
Polychromed plaster over welded steel
each approximately 5′9″ x 15½″ x 15½″

A QUESTION OF FAITH
The Sculpture of Ronald Gonzalez

Catalogue essay by
Rachael Sadinsky

May 1-30, 1987

RICHARD F. BRUSH ART GALLERY
St. Lawrence University, Canton, New York

Acknowledgments

Ronald Gonzalez's sculpture resists explanation or classification. Any analysis, while offering insight or perspective, will remain an opinion, or rather, one aspect. This catalogue, *A Question of Faith: The Sculpture of Ronald Gonzalez,* is my view. The catalogue and the accompanying exhibition of Gonzalez's recent work represent the fulfillment of my longstanding desire to work with the artist. I've known the sculptor for several years and continue to admire the profound commitment and the remarkable strength he brings to his art. His eagerness to participate in this project, his sensitive and candid answers to my often relentless questioning, and his trust and generosity have made the long hours of preparation a distinct pleasure. I am indebted to Geo Raica, director of Richard F. Brush Art Gallery, for his invaluable support, advice, and encouragement, all of which made the Gonzalez exhibition at St. Lawrence University and the catalogue possible. Finally, I wish to thank Kevin Ritter, assistant professor of theatre arts, for his perceptive comments on the text of the catalogue and his willingness to discuss the issues and consequences of, as he termed them, these "victims of The Day After."

Rachael Sadinsky
Curator, Brush Art Gallery

Copyright © 1987 Richard F. Brush Art Gallery
St. Lawrence University, Canton, NY   13617

Library of Congress Cataloguing-in-Publication Data

Sadinsky, Rachael, 1958-

A question of faith.

Bibliography: p.
1. Gonzalez, Ronald—Exhibitions.   2. Sculpture, American—Exhibitions.   3. Sculpture, Modern—20th century—United States—Exhibitions.   I. Richard F. Brush Art Gallery.   II. Title.
NB237.G625A4   1987   730′.92′4   87-4660
ISBN   0-933607-01-6

Foreword

An occasion imbued with the power and drama provided by the current installation of sculpture by Binghamton artist Ronald Gonzalez gives cause to reflect upon the Richard F. Brush Art Gallery's longstanding commitment to quality and to a wide range of aesthetic ideas. The recent renovation of the galleries affords the opportunity to pursue the nature and spirit of what we do in an arena carefully and collectively set aside for the "artistic experience." That this experience has been set aside is significant; we are thankful for an environment in which to question this nature and this spirit—that spirit which implodes our acts of faith in knowledge, and the criteria we use to gauge human growth and development.

The Gonzalez exhibition, with Curator Rachael Sadinsky's insightful scrutiny of the artist's work, is no exception to this faithful attempt to illuminate. Quite appropriately, Sadinsky earmarks the issue of faith as primary to understanding both the artist and his work. Certainly, the formalist blood in some way find itself at odds with these curious objects made of plaster, rags, and paint. These figures are particularly metaphorical to this viewer's eye and especially allusionistic in their literary impact, much in the same way that R.B. Kitaj's work activates one's imagination. Gonzalez gives us a body of work with such power and depth that the work speaks to us directly, immediately, and humanistically: what the existential writers have explored as the human condition, the tragic flaw, the awareness of being aware; the Janovian primal scream; a Bacon-esque experience; the disconnection Tillach speaks of as Sin; and the experience Sadinsky implies in her opening reference to Eliot's *The Hollow Men*. Gonzalez not only fabricates perplexing objects out of impermanent, perishable material, but also orchestrates ghost sculptures that are the ethereal remnants of a derelict state of spiritual disintigration, ultimate "still lives," tendentious swatches of absurd tragi-comedy brought to an eternal halt in the pre-dawn of living, spiritual reconciliation.

This installation is a cathartic performance piece that evokes a symbolic Cold War stalemate at Armegeddon. These disenfranchised figures are a reductionist's siege on Camus's *The Stranger*; fossilized expatriates of disenchantment; a subjective, iconoclastic, stop-action narrative of fugitive artifacts which reflect the poetic resonance of Everyman's hallucinatory spiritual decomposition. One can perceive where particular Freudian and Jungian enthusiasts of the Collective Unconscious, the notion of Art's need to transcend "time and material," and art critic Donald Kuspit's concern with the preconscious order of effects, could substantiate their place in this artist's domain. Even our advocates of mystical realism and our surrealists will find themselves at home within the sturdy framework of Gonzalez's metaphysical life-structure.

The Richard F. Brush Art Gallery takes pleasure in featuring an appraisal of an important artist. I want to thank both Rachael Sadinsky and Ronald Gonzalez for their tireless efforts on this project.

Geo Raica
Director, Brush Art Gallery

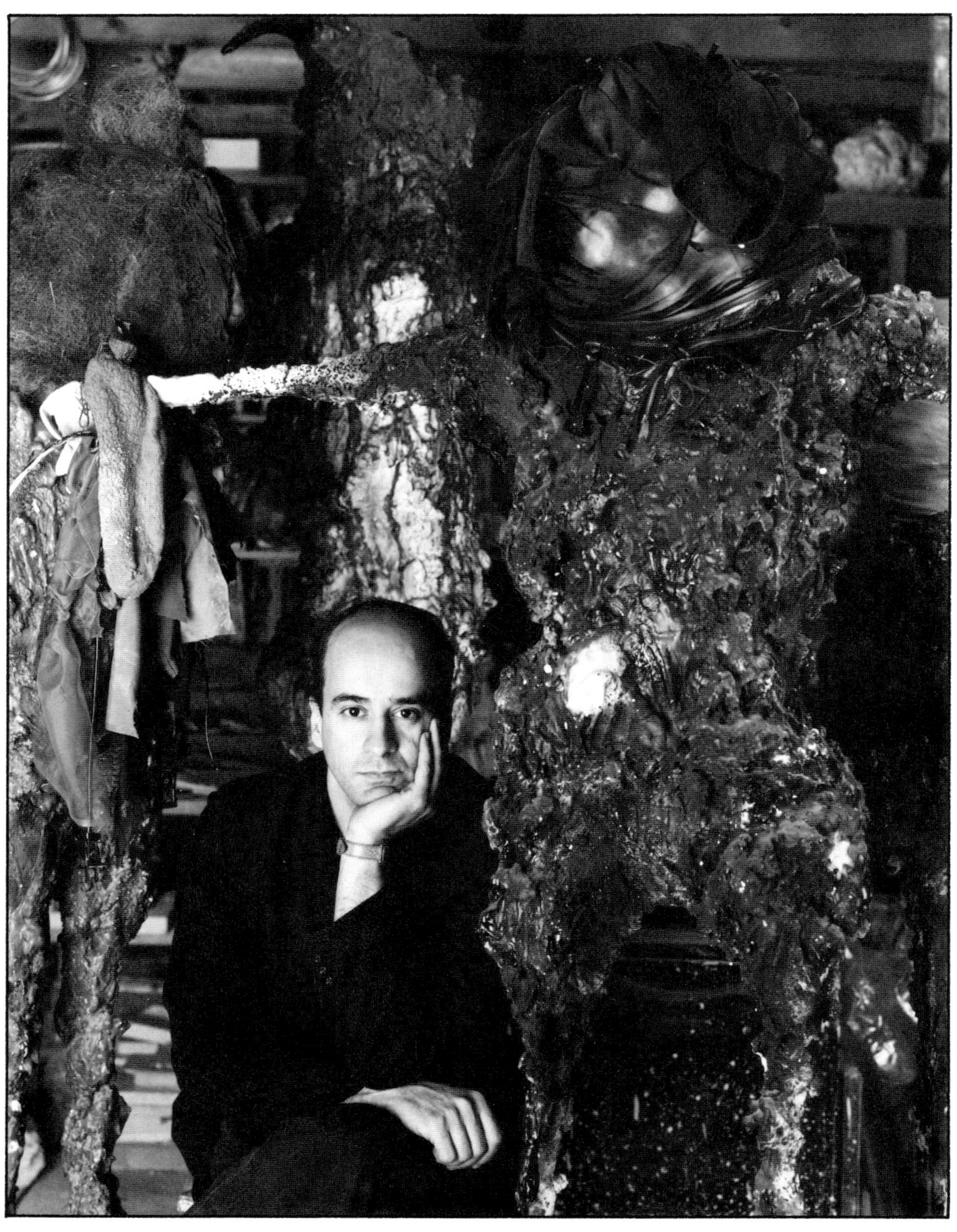

2. Gonzalez in his studio, 1987

Is it like this
In death's other kingdom
Waking alone
At the hour when we are
Trembling with tenderness
Lips that would kiss
Form prayers to broken stone.

T.S. Eliot
The Hollow Men

Ronald Gonzalez is a prolific sculptor, one who has created an entire race of plaster figures ranging from the tiny in reliefs and assemblages to the monumental in free-standing form. At the heart of his concerns, however, is not merely the human form but, more importantly, the human soul, a concept that never seems to lose its fascination for him. His recent sculptures are lifesize, polychromed plaster figures with oversized heads, gouged-out eyes, and attenuated spindly legs. These figures are often without arms and most are shrouded, some in bondage. They stand immobile, helpless and unable to be helped, each alone in his suffering. These are desperate figures, embodiments of trouble, sin, death and dying. They seem to wonder why and to fear what may or may not come next. With these figures, the artist asks those uncomfortable, if not terrifying, questions about man's existence. Through his work, Gonzalez challenges the viewer to question long-accepted principles and beliefs about the meaning of life and of death. Those with unsteady faith proceed with caution. Those without faith cringe with the realizations which come to easily.

The artist's personal sense of history, or, if you will, the spirit of place, informs his work and shapes his vision. Born, raised, and educated in or near Binghamton, New York, the artist has rarely ventured far from home. Gonzalez has deep emotional ties to the area; his current studio is on the site of his late father's used car lot and adjacent to his mother's house. As the artist has stated, "So many ghosts underneath my feet . . . I've travelled far in Binghamton . . . dreams, places, a million barstools."[1] The artist is supersitious of moving. The daily confrontation between past and present is the source of his inspiration and the cause of his torment as a child's memories and fears rub shoulders with an adult's tragedies and triumphs. Gonzalez's sculptures are born of his roots in Binghamton; however, they are not limited to it: reconciling old beliefs and truths with new realizations and circumstances is a struggle we all must endure as part of maturity. It is for this reason his sculpture is so compelling.

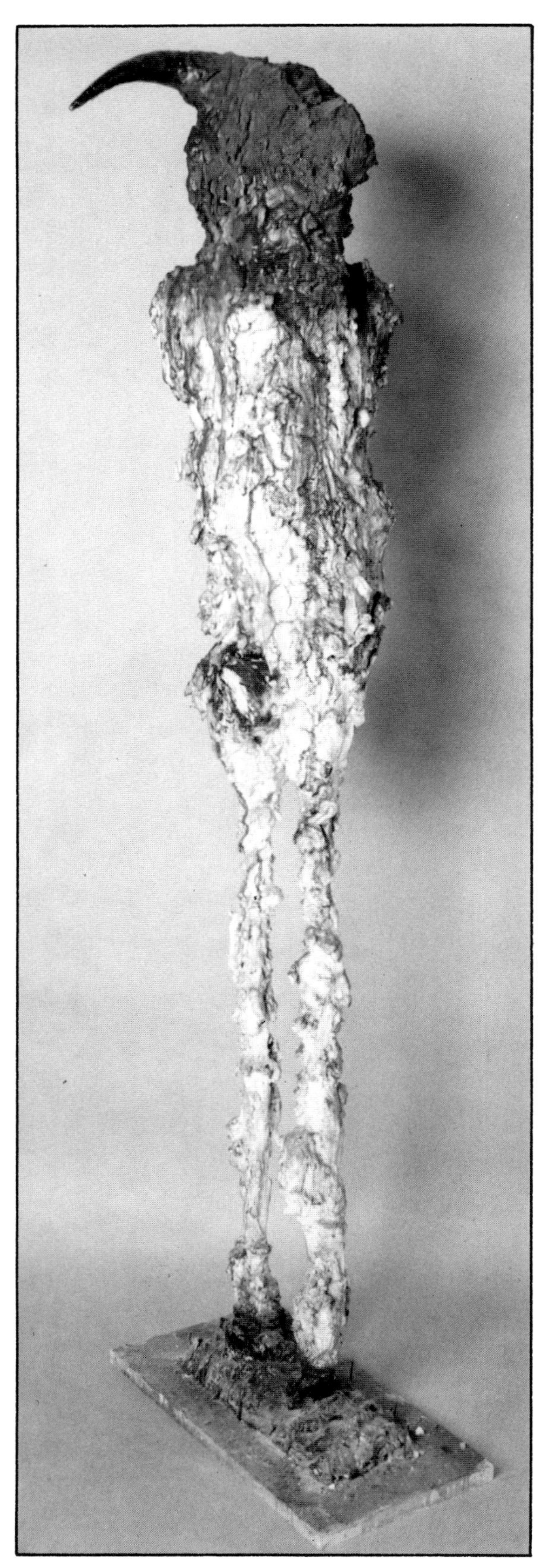

3. ***Horned Figure***, 1987
   Polychromed plaster with mixed media
   over welded steel
   7′3″ x 26½″ x 19″

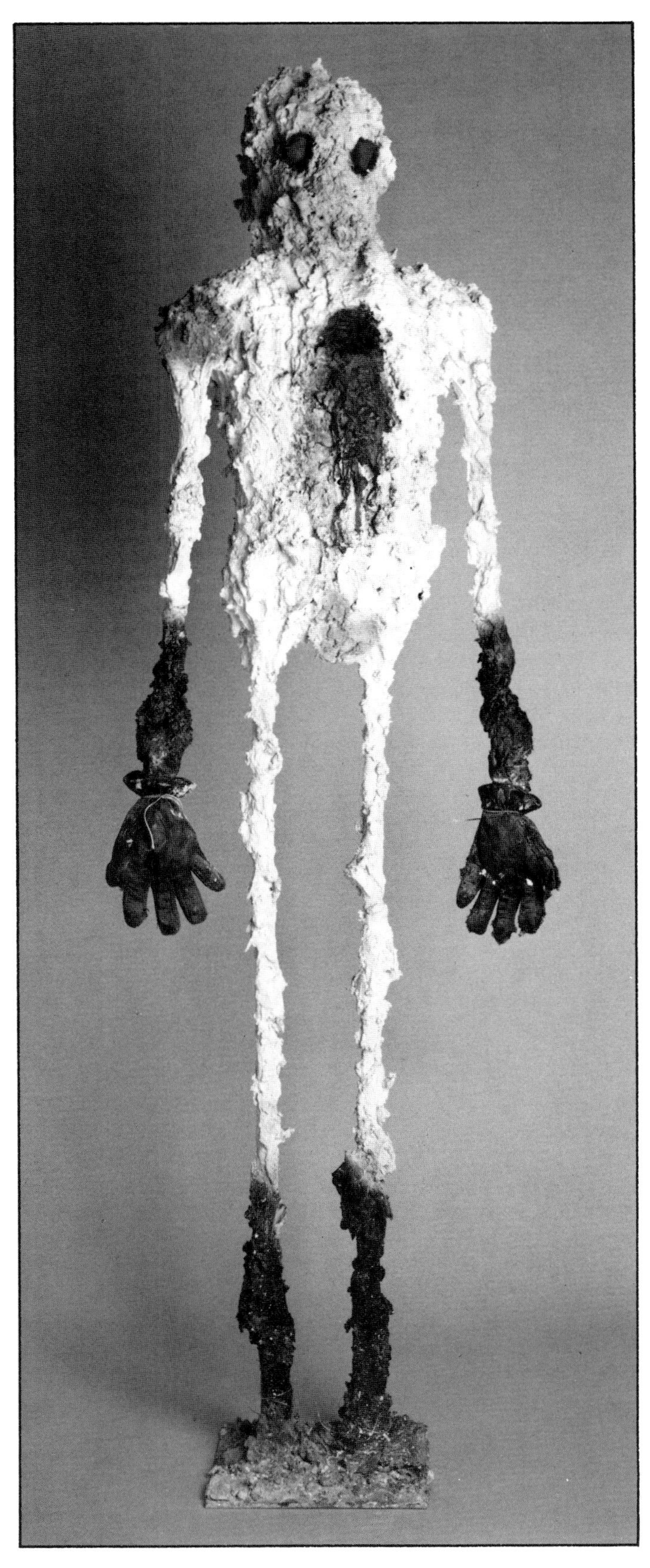

4. *Figure (Red Gush)*, 1986
    Polychromed plaster with mixed media
    over welded steel
    6′6″ x 25″ x 14″

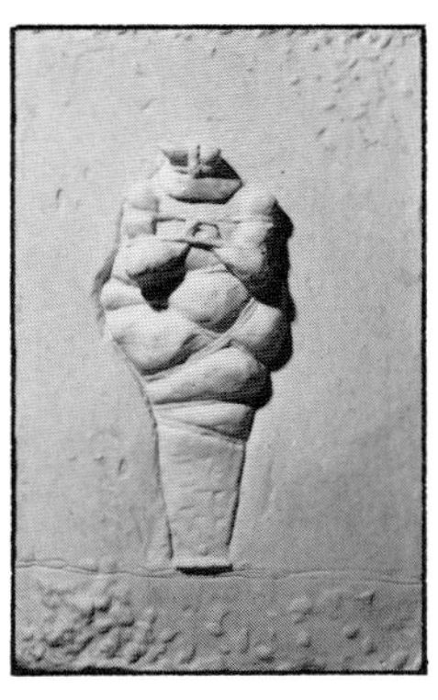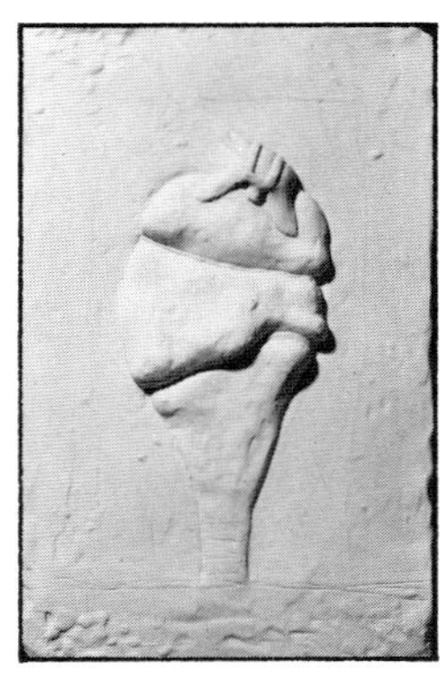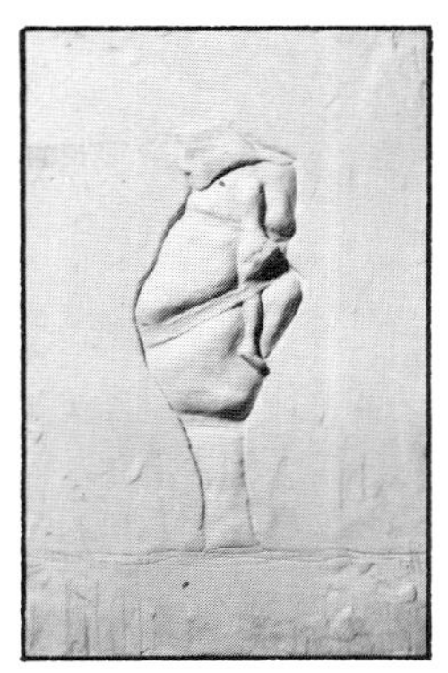

5. ***Untitled Reliefs #3, #4, and #5***
(from a series of 7), 1979
Plaster
each 13½″ x 8¾″

Gonzalez's obsession with sculpture, in particular, with awe-inspiring iconic figures, began at a young age. As a child, he attended Catholic school and was facinated with the sculptures stored in the church basement where he "pretended to be the artist of these abandoned saints and Virgins."[2] Gonzalez often made toys out of found objects; for example, a collection of bottle caps was transformed into a fleet of ships. During these years, he amassed a trinket collection in order to create his very own personal, very controlled tableaux, a practice he retained in both form and intent in his latter-day assemblages. In the early 1970s, Gonzalez worked with the Harpursville stonecarver Genevieve Hamlin. With her advice and support, he experimented with a variety of techniques and materials, including stone and wood carving and modeling clay. His small reclining and seated figures of this period are reminiscent of the monumental forms of Henry Moore, but on a more manageable scale. His formal training began in the latter part of the decade, when he enrolled in the fine arts program at SUNY-Binghamton. A life drawing class with Don DeMauro and, in particular, exposure to DeMauro's figurative paintings and drawings prompted Gonzalez's work with fragmentary figurative imagery. In Ed Wilson's life sculpture course, Gonzalez received technical direction, especially for plaster casting, and Wilson's encouragement to continue in figurative sculpture. His plaster reliefs of 1979 and 1980 (fig. 3) document DeMauro's influence but also recall Rodin and his interest in the figural fragment: hanging in Gonzalez's apartment is a timeworn photograph of Rodin's studio at Meudon containing shelves and drawers of *membra disjecta,* an assortment of plaster fragments, arms, legs, noses, et al., that were used, exchanged, or discarded during the creation of *The Gates of Hell.*

In the late 1970s through the early 1980s, Gonzalez worked almost exclusively with plaster, making reliefs, small figures, and assemblages. The artist chose to work in the fragile medium of plaster precisely because of its vulnerability and its susceptibility to being damaged, a fate similar to that of the human body itself. Gonzalez's distortion of the figure, albeit on a small scale, is disturbing to look at (figs. 5-7). Deformed, crippled figures are depicted in bondage, heads and bodies hang suspended, mouths utter voiceless screams. When more than one figure is depicted (fig. 8), we are presented with an indistinct mass of bodies. With their chorus of moans, the agonizing heads and darkened eye sockets beg our sympathy.

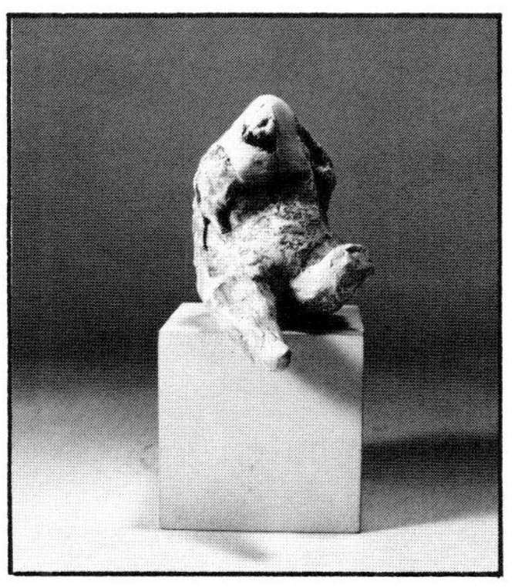
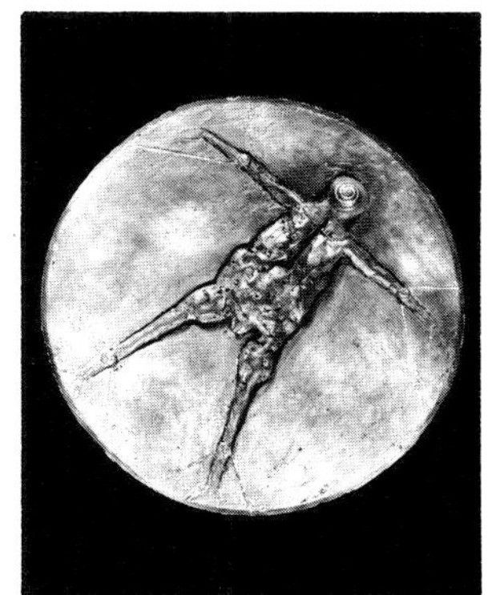
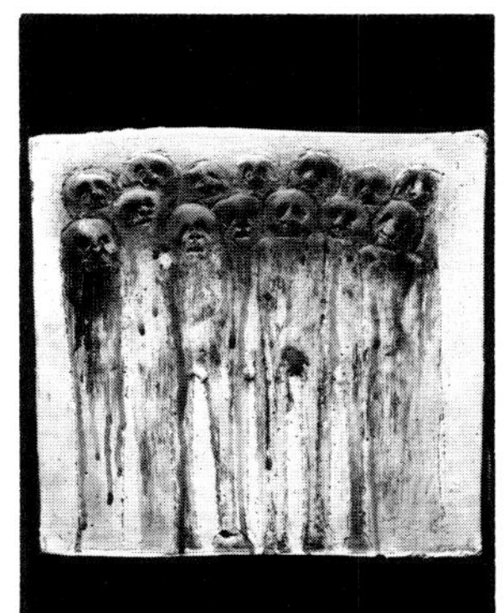

6. *Seated Figure,* 1980
Polychromed plaster
8¾″ x 4″ x 5½″
Private Collection

7. *Relief Study-Target,* 1981
Polychromed plaster
11¾″ x 11¾″ x ⅞″
Private Collection

8. *Crowd,* 1983
Polychromed plaster
11½″ x 11½″ x 1″

Many of these works incorporate found objects to underscore and further enhance the significance of the work. *Time Bomb* (fig. 10), for example, is an armless ghoul with bits of wire and plastic where a brain and eyes should be. Gonzalez's collection of found objects is a reflection of his love for the tiny and his attraction for "the forgotten, lost, homeless, mutilated, broken, holy, and damned."[4] He scrounges second-hand and thrift stores for tiny skeletons and skulls, plastic dolls, religious artifacts, buttons, bones, watch crystals, magazines—in short, anything that is, in a very real sense, priceless. The artist makes creative use of both the form and content of these cheap, mass-produced toys or disposable garbage. Real artifacts from our world afford a point of departure and serve as known signs and symbols in the artist's exploration into the unknown. By offering recognizable guideposts, the artist makes it easier and more palatable for us to accompany him on a voyage to a grotesque, forbidden land where nothing is sacred and everything is under scrutiny.

A random sample of his titles indicates that a significant portion of Gonzalez's work is concerned with religious iconography or themes: *Do Roses Bloom In Heaven; Crucifixion; Now I Lay Me Down To Sleep; Ashes To Ashes; Looking Unto Jesus; Christmas Crucifixion; Once You Get To Heaven You Can Never Get Out; Sacred Heart Shrine; The Devil; The Devil Meets The Little White Church;* to name a few. A survey of the reliefs reveals a preference for a tri-partite organization, either in the tradition-laden triptych format or in a cross-sectional structure depicting heaven and hell with "reality" in between. Recollections of his religious upbringing and of his many years in Catholic school and as an altarboy indicate that Gonzalez's most profound memory is of the religion's history of spiritual torture, the many martyrdoms, the notion of hell and the requisite emphasis on the devil. On a trip to Italy in 1983, the artist was both fascinated and appalled by the bloodiness of religious art in the churches; the graphic stigmatas and martyrdoms depicted in these holy sites only increased Gonzalez's obsession with the more horrific aspects of the religion. The relief *Somebody Died By Somebody's Hand* (fig. 9) is a nightmarish reconstruction of a traditional crucifixion scene: the marytred body/skeleton is on the cross under God the Father's sign of the hand. Below is a cross-section of skulls, all the "ghosts" under our feet. As Paula Rea Radisch perceptively noted, in Gonzalez's view there is no redemption: the hand is bloodied, death is merely physical extinction and holds no promise of spiritual release.[5]

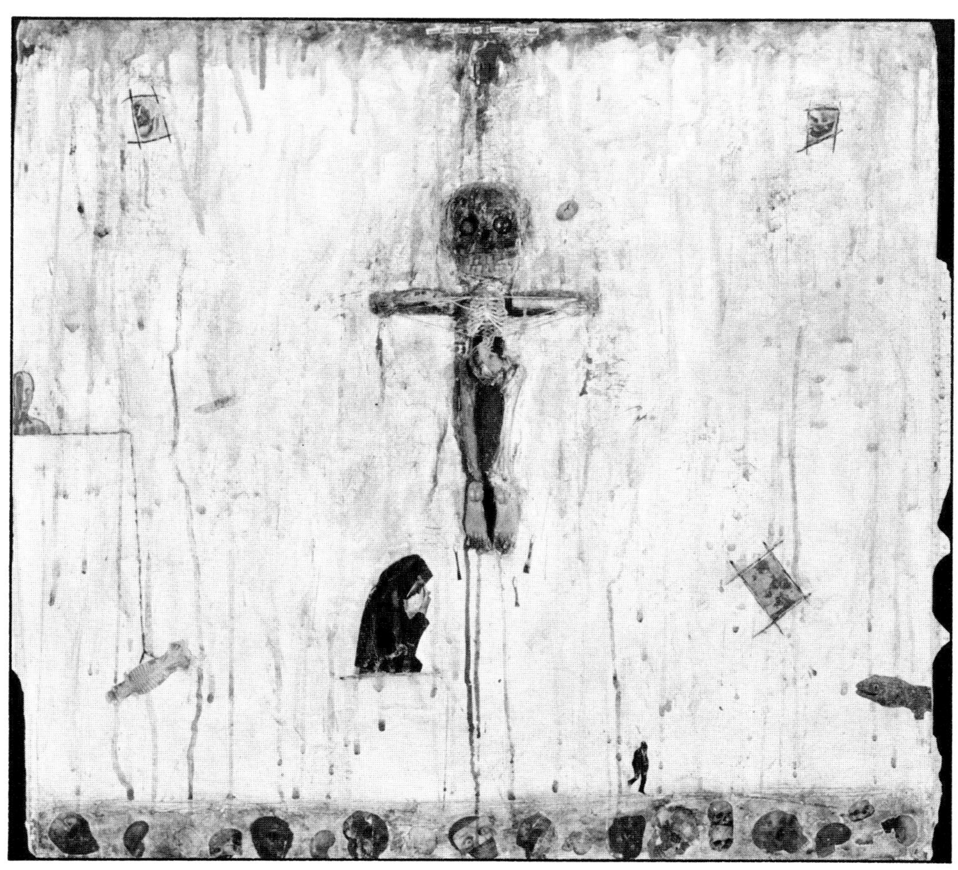

9. ***Somebody Died By Somebody's Hand***, 1984
Plaster with mixed media
25½″ x 29″ x 1½″

The assemblages are the artist's most idiosyncratic response to life, its terrors and its injustices. Gonzalez is extremely protective of the assemblages because of their fragility as well as their personal iconography and graphic imagery. Fabrication does not eliminate terrors, but it does, at least, objectify them so that they can be confronted. *You Must Have Been A Beautiful Baby* (fig. 15) depicts a cherubic face encapsulated in a blackened clump of a head with chipped teeth and wispy gray hair. A jewelled beaded bow on a lace scrap is substituted for a dress and adorns this decrepit stick figure. The assemblage presents a frightening illustration of the delusions of youthful glory that we perpetuate, hoping to delay the inevitable and bitter reality of aging and dying. *Christmas Crucifixion* (fig. 16) is a cruciform shape surmounted with an image of Christ's face and gaily decorated with tiny Christmas decorations and tinsel. The assemblage is an elegant example of Gonzalez's art of contradiction: he commemorates Christ's birth with an image of his death.

In his recent work, the simplicity and scale are initially the most surprising (figs. 1-4, 11-14, 17 and 18). Accustomed to Gonzalez's intricately complex assemblages and reliefs, these lifesize or larger figures have an overpowering presence. The attenuated legs seem too painfully thin to support the bulky

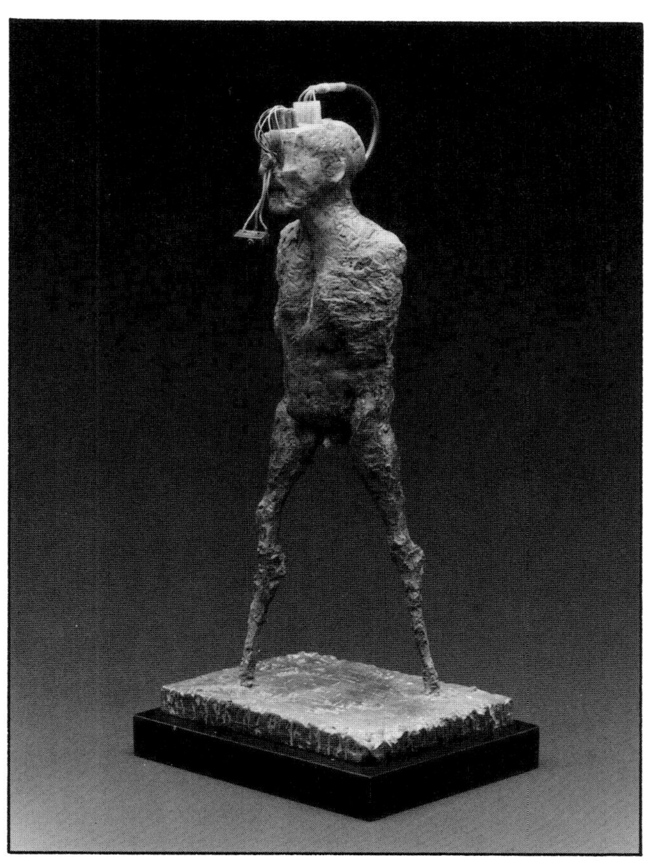

10. ***Time Bomb,*** 1981
Polychromed plaster with mixed media
over welded steel
16½″ x 8″ x 6″

torsos and disproportionate heads. The plaster skin is left deliberately rough
and furrowed, and color is applied to heighten certain features: bulging or
gouged-out eyes; a gaping hole in the chest; charred ankles. Most are without
arms; one has disfigured hands covered with ragged workman's gloves.
Several of the massive heads are covered with filmy, gauzy scarves, offering a
softened, discretely hidden identity that contrasts with the brutal appearance
of the body. These intimidating figures demand direct confrontation. They
stand in our space, they stare at us, pleading to be recognized and understood
despite their repelling appearances. These are gruesome victims of The Day
After, wretched creatures unable to get beyond the delicate haze enclosing
their over-developed brains and imagined securities. Those who do "see" and
"feel" display their horribly mutilated and scarred bodies without remorse.
These figures inhabit a painful world where belief in a just and secure life and
afterlife is transplanted with a terrifying reality and the utter finality of death.
Gonzalez's grotesque creatures assault our twentieth-century sensibilities and
our post-spiritual sensitivities. We turn away, too repulsed to stare, too
morbidly intrigued to ignore, unable to forget.

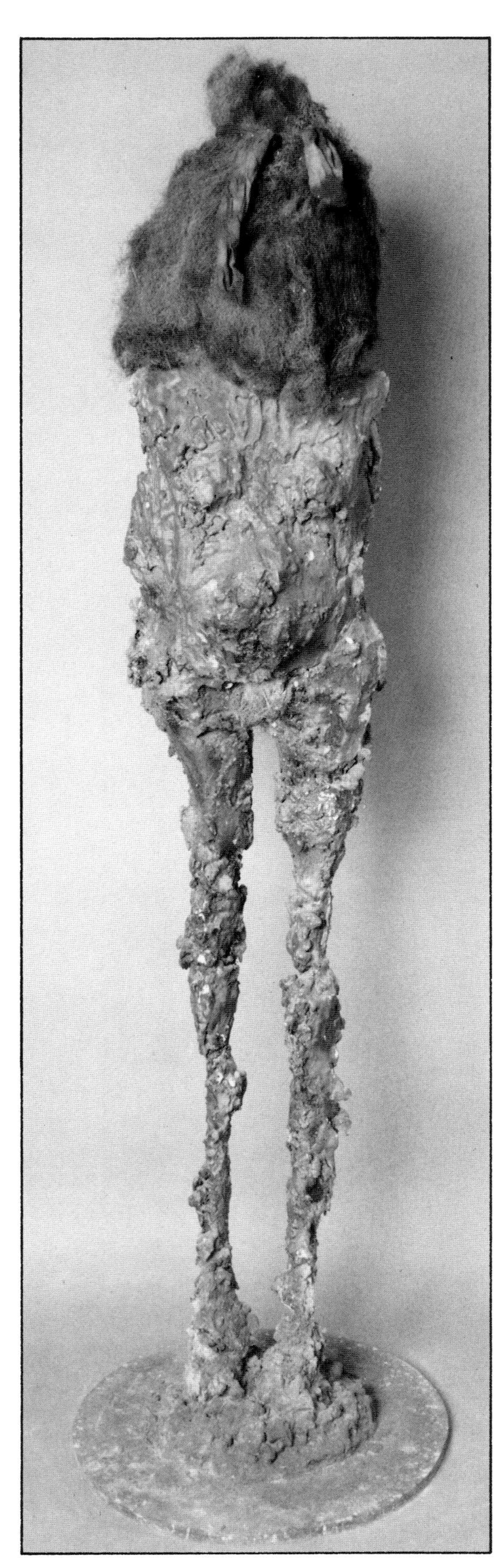

11. ***Blue Women,*** 1987
    Polychromed plaster with mixed media
    over welded steel
    6'8" x 24" x 24"

Gonzalez's work contains references to and similarities with artists in the tradition of figural sculpture, Rodin, Giacometti, and, of course, Michelangelo, who created works that had a function and identity as sculpture and not necessarily as true replicas of the human form. Gonzalez's work recalls, in particular, the approach and handling of Giacometti's attenuated figures that express an elementary existential questioning of human identity and purpose. More contemporary influences include the nightmarish figures of Edward Keinholz and Canadian artist Mark Prent. Their lifesize and lifelike fiberglass figures derive from man's morbid attraction for the grotesque, with death and infirmity, with the victimized and distorted. Their audience is both disturbed and intrigued by the startling three-dimensional reality and presence and then terrified by an all-too-apparent similarity to these poor creatures.

This fascination with the "grotesque" has a long history in art: the word itself derives from the Italian *grottesco*, the ornamental style found in the fifteenth-century excavations of Roman ruins. In the ensuing centuries, the meaning of grotesque encompassed something playfully gay and fantastic as well as sinister and ominous. In the eighteenth century, the term was applied to caricatures which imitated a distorted and ugly reality by exaggerating existing situations. Imagined monstrosities were created without losing their foundation in reality. By the twentieth century, the grotesque lost its playful connotation entirely, and became solely an instrument of terrifying or ominous overtones. To the modern viewer, the grotesque has enough similarities to our world to raise doubts and questions about our comfortable and safe reality. As Wolfgang Kayser explains:

> The Grotesque is the estranged world . . . it is our world which has to be transformed . . . Our world ceases to be reliable, and we feel we would be unable to live in this changed world. The grotesque instills fear of life rather than fear of death.[6]

The grotesque in art has a cathartic effect: after the shock of the initial view, we curiously inspect and examine the work that contains such power. Finally we experience a numbed reconciliation by attempting to find meaning, to find relevance, to quiet the awful terrors incited by the work. In short, regardless of how repulsed we may be by a grotesque image, we cannot avoid coming to terms with it. According to Geoffrey Harpham, the grotesque breaks the complacency of superficial reality, thereby enabling one to see and perhaps to understand underlying truths:

> Fragmented, jumbled, or corrupted representation leads us into the grotesque; and it leads us out of it as well, generating the interpretive activity that seeks closure, either in the discovery of a novel form or in a metaphysical, analogical, or allegorical explanation.[7]

The grotesque, by virtue of its power to shock, permits a degree of self-discovery, and the temporary confusion and disorder is but a small price to pay for knowledge.

Art that is deliberately "ugly" finds an audience only with difficulty. Grotesque art is especially alienating because it challenges the viewer to question accepted principles. Goya's attraction for the grotesque, evident in, for example, *Los Caprichos* or *La Tauromachia*, allowed him to satirize Spanish society. Artists who choose a grotesque approach as a means of exploring man's identity and purpose use their art as a form of existential exorcism. Such work has an appearance of a morbid longing for negativity and a denial of faith. In short, grotesque art is spiritually threatening and dangerous. However, it may be more accurate to describe artists of the grotesque as having courageously accepted negativity. Their act of challenging faith is not denying it but rather evidence of some sort of belief. Paul Tillich believes that being "concerned about one's own being, about one's self and one's world, about its meaning and its estrangement and its finitude" is a broad definition of religion.[8] Furthermore, as Carl Skrade maintains, so-called "grotesque" art may be a way of discovering or confirming faith in the artist and especially in the viewer:

> Perhaps the grotesque can force us to hear the inaudible word that can speak to us in our vacuum, our time between times, of new and viable images and symbols which can help to thrust us beyond the bomb and beyond 1984.[9]

Gonzalez's apocalyptic visions are an experiment in and a test of the option of faith in our Brave New World. By mediating his present through his past, Gonzalez summons up and gives shape to fears and terrors that torment all of us. His grotesque figures are a product of our society's deteriorating physical environment, the unrelenting strangeness of our culture, and man's freakish and absurd nature. We resist the sculptures because we do not want certain issues regarding the meaning of life and the consequences of death dragged out and displayed before us so unrepentantly. His sculptures shake our comfortable assumptions and sanity-preserving deceptions. They take us to the brink of emotional black holes where most of us fear to go and then abandon us to find our way back to our lives, our rationalizations. How we return is of no concern to the artist. It is up to us, to sort out how these potent images are to be reconciled with beliefs and perceived truths. Gonzalez's mission is to raise the issues of our identity and purpose and to explore their consequences on our existence. Gonzalez creates religious art for our troubled times.

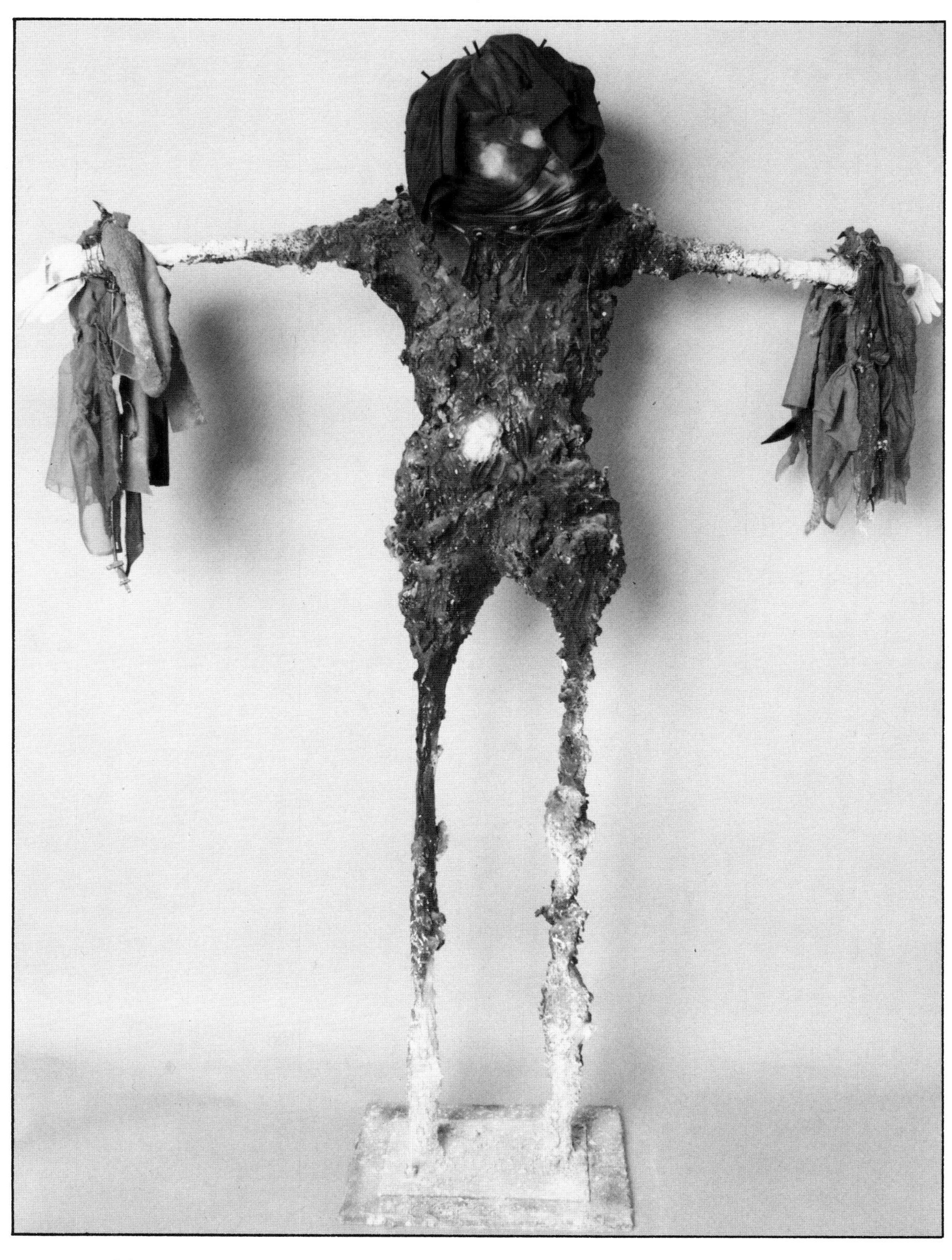

12. ***Man of Sorrows,*** 1987
    Polychromed plaster with mixed media
    over welded steel
    6′6″ x 5′8″ x 16″

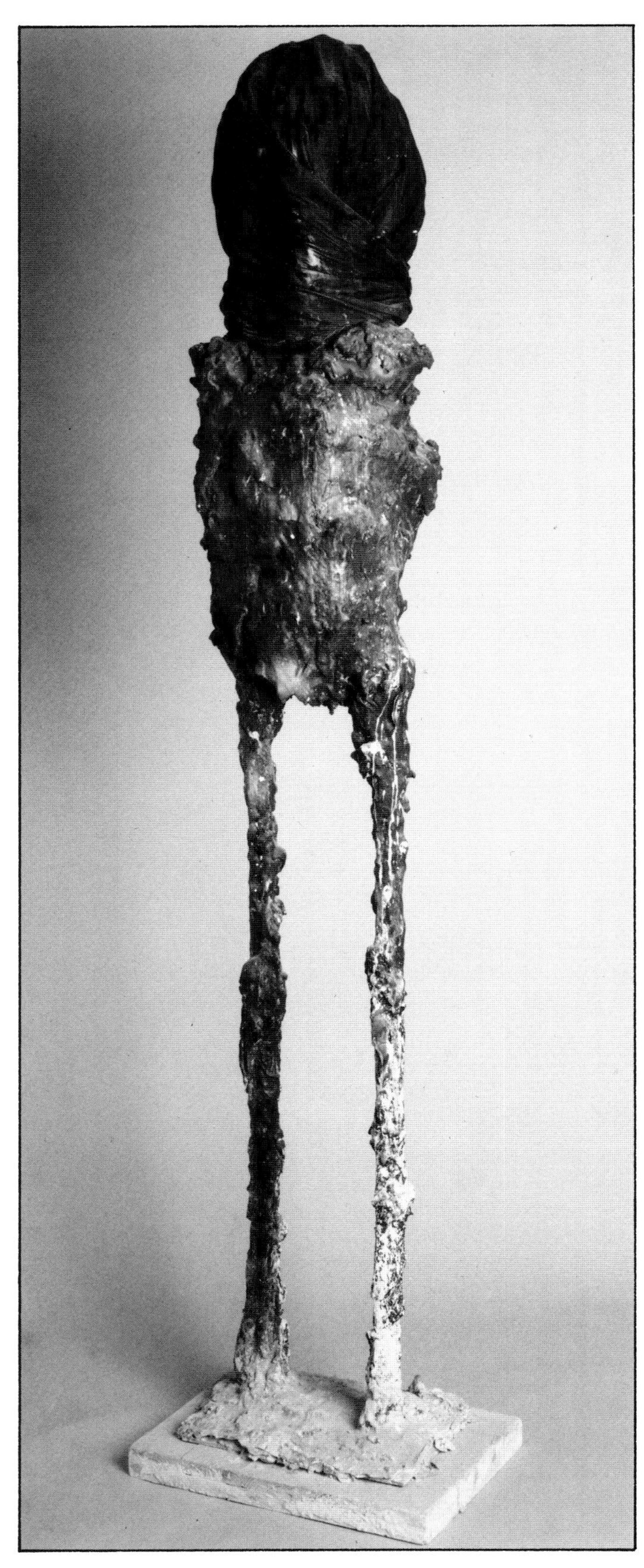

13. ***Black Figure***, 1985-86
Polychromed plaster with mixed media
over welded steel
6'7" x 17¼" x 13"

Footnotes

1. These and succeeding statements in which I've quoted the artist are taken from an informal interview and lengthy conversations between the author and the artist in late October, 1986, and early January, 1987.

2. *Ibid.*

3. Photographs of Rodin's studio at Meudon may be found in Albert Elsen, *Rodin* (New York: Museum of Modern Art, 1963) on page 176. Elsen's discussion of Rodin's use of plaster fragments in the making of *The Gates of Hell* is found on pages 174-175.

4. *Op. cit.*

5. The relief *Somebody Died By Somebody's Hand* was included in an exhibition entitled *Vinculos (Connections): Latin American Mysticism/North American Materialism* at the Mendenhall Gallery, Whittier College, Whittier, California, in October, 1986, and was discussed in the accompanying catalogue in a foreword by Dr. Radisch.

6. Wolfgang Kayser, *The Grotesque in Art and Literature*, trans. Ulrich Weisstein (New York: McGraw-Hill Book Company, 1966), pp. 184-185.

7. Geoffrey Galt Harpham, *On the Grotesque: Strategies of Contradiction in Art and Literature* (Princeton: Princeton University Press, 1982), p. 18.

8. Paul Tillich, "Existential Aspects of Modern Art," *Christianity and the Existentialists*, ed. Carl Michalson (New York: Charles Scribner's Sons, 1956), p. 132.

9. Carl Skrade, *God and the Grotesque* (Philadelphia: Westminster Press, 1974), p. 18.

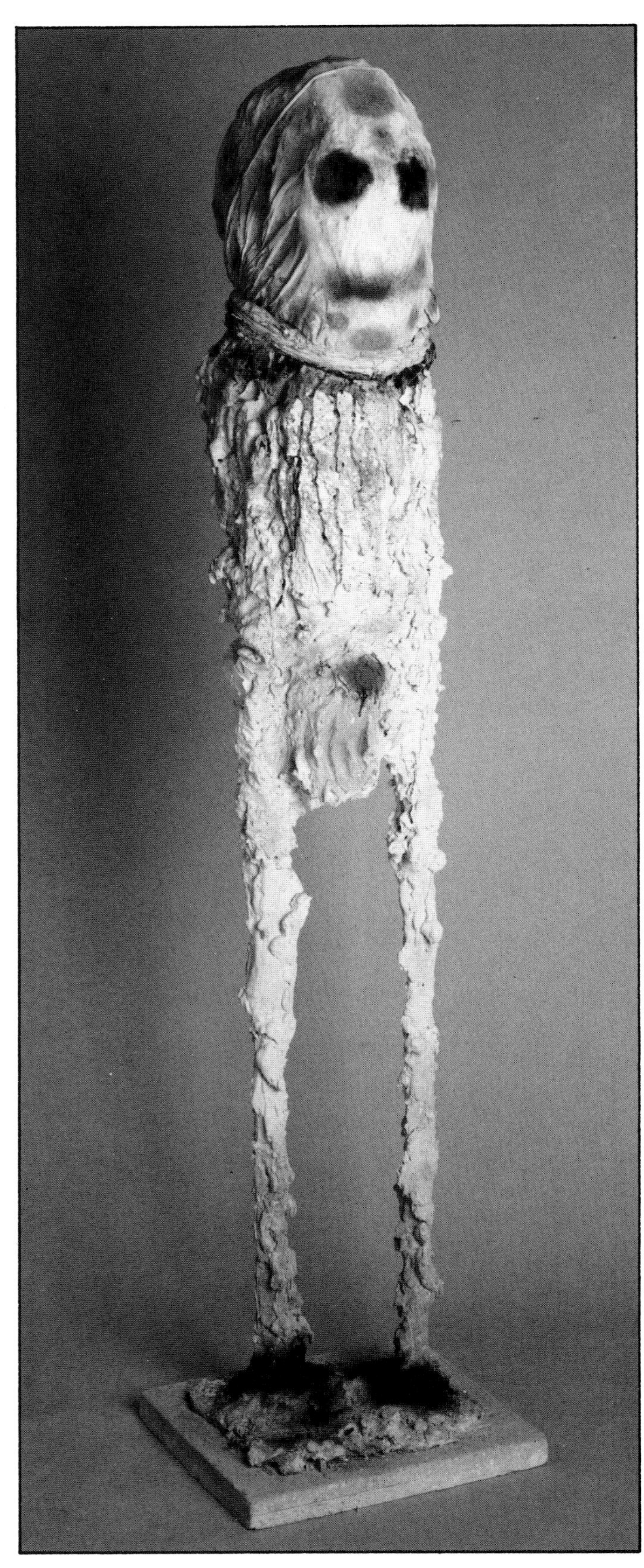

14. ***Ghost Figure***, 1985-86
Polychromed plaster with mixed media
over welded steel
6′6″ x 25″ x 14″

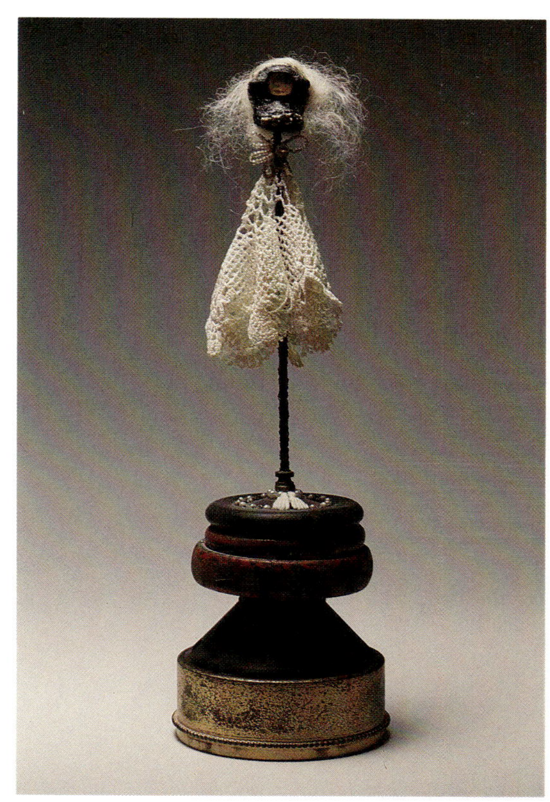

15. ***You Must Have Been A Beautiful Baby,*** 1983
    Mixed media assemblage
    13″ x 4″ x 4″

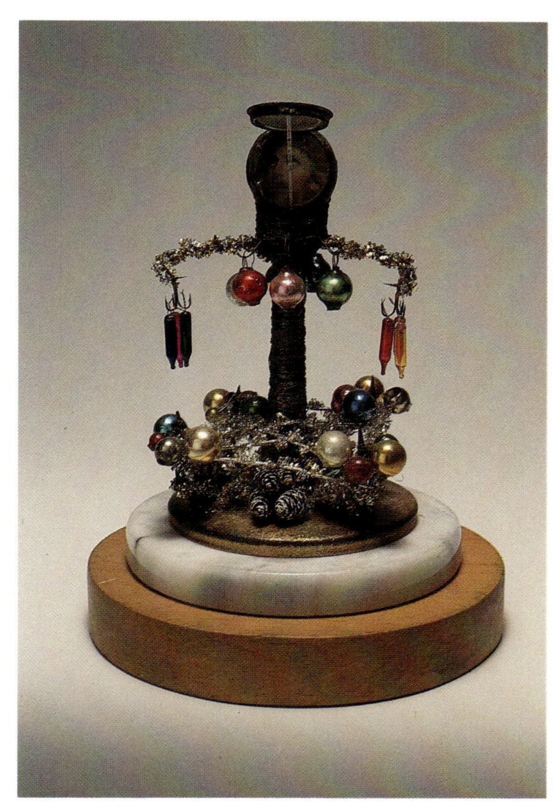

16. ***Christmas Crucifixion***, 1984
    Mixed media assemblage
    8½″ x 7″ x 7″

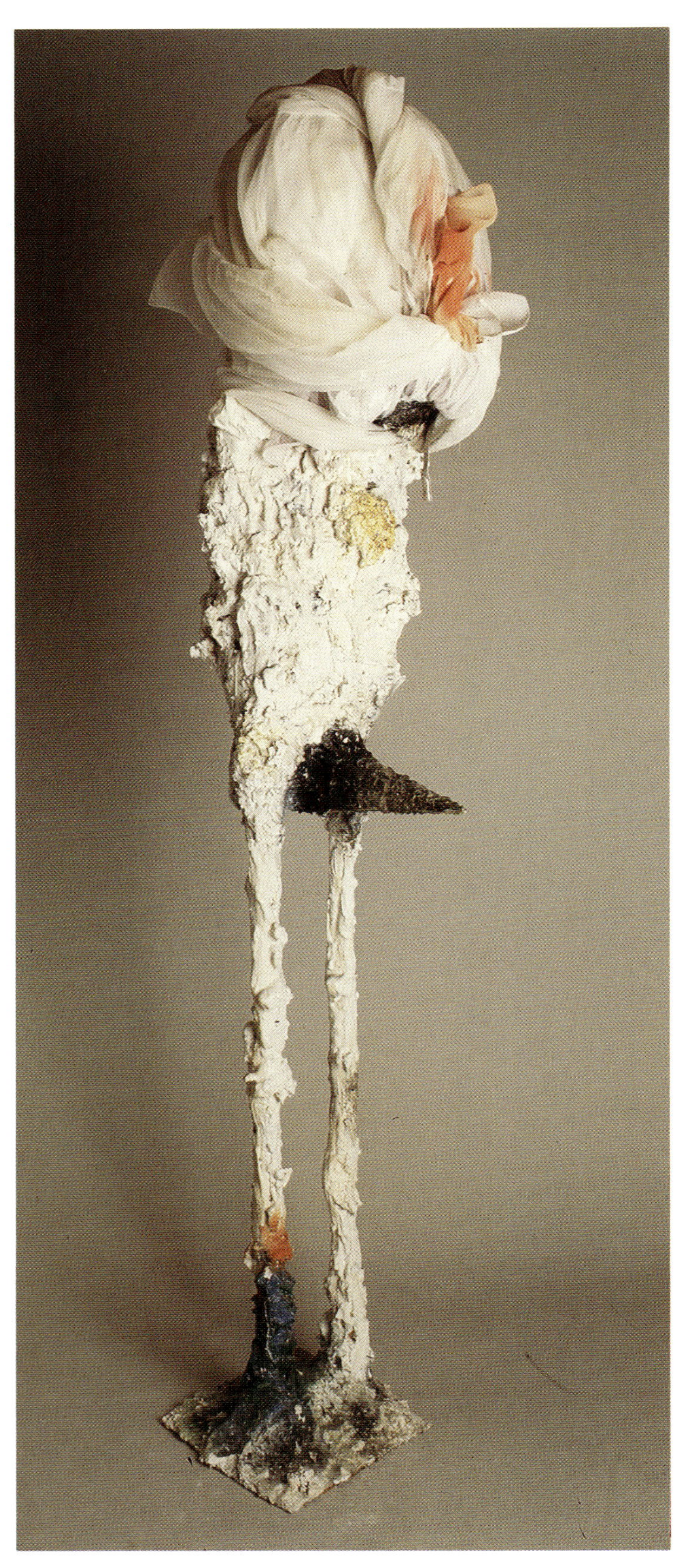

17. *Figure (Stinger)*, 1986
Polychromed plaster with mixed media
over welded steel
6'9" x 19" x 26"

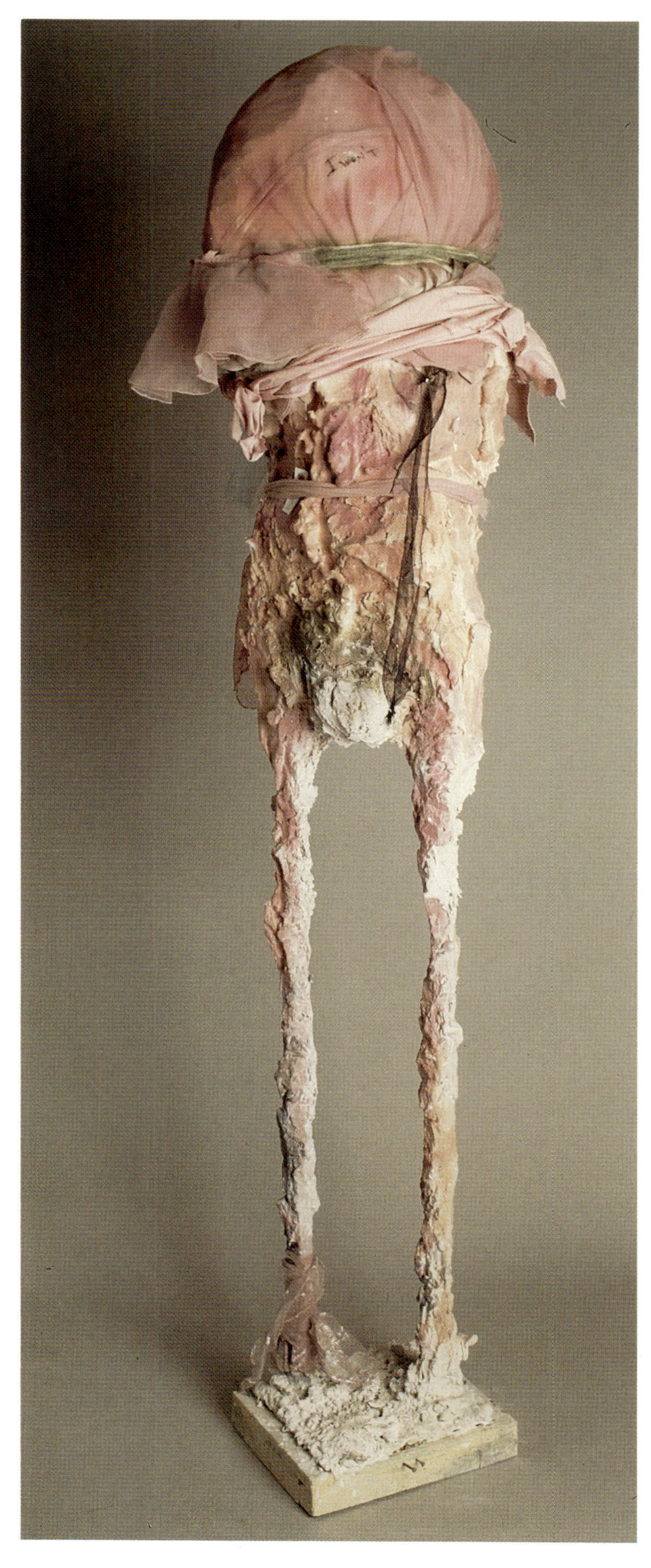

18. ***Pink Figure for C.R.***
(Don't Ruin the Pink Figure), 1986
Polychromed plaster with mixed media
6'6" x 25" x 14"

Photography by Bruce Wrighton, except figs. 6-8 by Rachael Sadinsky
Catalogue design by Greg Mark and Rachael Sadinsky
Typography by Tracy L. Robertson, University Relations, St. Lawrence University
Printing by Finger Lakes Press, Auburn, New York